WONDERFUL
WORLD OF
ANIMALS

This 1997 edition published by Brockhampton Press
20 Bloomsbury Street, London WC1B 3QA

Text by Beatrice MacLeod
Designed by Marco Nardi
Illustrated by Umberta Pezzuoli

Created and produced by McRae Books Srl
Via dei Rustici, 5 – Florence, Italy

ISBN 1-86019-585-7

WONDERFUL WORLD OF ANIMALS

REPTILES

Beatrice MacLeod
Illustrated by Umberta Pezzuoli

BROCKHAMPTON PRESS

WHAT IS A REPTILE?

Reptiles include crocodiles, turtles, snakes and lizards. All reptiles have scales and breathe through their lungs. Unlike birds and mammals, which have constant body temperatures, a reptile adapts its temperature to the environment in which it lives.

4

Tortoises and turtles have hard shells to protect their bodies. The horny shell, or shield, is rounded and attached to the soft, flat underside. Their toothless mouths have a cutting bony ridge, as sharp as a beak.

Atlantic sea turtle

Crocodiles spend most of their lives in the water. They use their tails to swim. They have long snouts and strong jaws with sharp teeth, to catch unsuspecting prey.

Nile crocodile

Snakes have long slender bodies covered in scaly skin. They can measure anywhere from 10 centimetres to 10 metres in length. Most snakes have poor eyesight; they recognize other animals by vibrations of the ground or by smell.

Leopard snake

Movement

The word 'reptile' comes from Latin and means 'creeping' or 'crawling'. Snakes have no legs and they slither along the ground. But many reptiles can also swim, run or even glide through the air!

Tortoises have short toes for walking on land. Aquatic turtles have long toes with webbing to help them swim.

Matamata

The **Matamata**, a South American river turtle, walks along the bottom of the river underwater.

The **flying dragon**, a small Southeast Asian lizard, is one of the few reptiles that can 'fly'.

Flying dragon

By opening out a thin fold of skin along its sides, it makes gliding leaps of up to 14 metres at a time.

Fast and slow

Speed is useful for defence and hunting. In the water some turtles can hurtle along at 25 km/h! The race runner lizard in America was also timed at 25 km/h. The tortoise moves very slowly, but with its protective shell and patient hunting methods this is not a problem.

LAND REPTILES

Although there are some reptiles in most habitats, the majority of species live in the warm tropical areas of the Earth. Generally speaking, the farther from the equator you are, the fewer the reptiles you will encounter.

The **frilled lizard** lives in the arid grasslands of Australia. When threatened by a predator a collar of skin around its neck rises, making it look much bigger and scarier than it really is.

Australian frilled lizard

Huge, heavy and slow-moving, the **giant tortoise** lives on the islands of Galapagos (a Spanish word, meaning 'tortoise'), in the Pacific Ocean. The tortoises originally came from South America or the East Indies.

Galapagos giant tortoise

Emerald boa

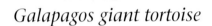

The **emerald boa** lives in the tropical rain forests of South America. Hidden in the branches, almost invisible among the bright green leaves, it waits for prey. It is not poisonous, and kills its victims with its huge front fangs.

AQUATIC REPTILES

Many reptiles, including sea turtles, crocodiles and some snakes and lizards live and feed mainly in the water. However, like almost all reptiles, they breed on land. Only a few species spend their whole lives in the water.

The **gharial**, a ferocious predator, is a species of crocodile. It lives in the great rivers of India. It has a long thin snout with sharp pointed teeth which it uses to catch its prey.

Gharial

Many snakes can swim, but only a few live in the water. The **sea krait** is a marine snake. It has valve-like closings on its nostrils so that it can breathe underwater. It does not come ashore, and produces live young at sea.

11

Endangered reptiles

Many species of reptiles, including crocodiles, alligators, monitor lizards and turtles, are in danger of becoming extinct. Their skins and shells are much sought after to make shoes, belts, bags, wallets and other fashion accessories.

FOOD AND FEEDING

Most reptiles are carnivores. They eat flesh, including birds, frogs, insects, fish, other reptiles and even large mammals. Some snakes can swallow prey much larger than themselves. Only a few species of iguana and some tortoises are herbivores (plant-eaters).

The **marine iguana**, a large lizard that lives on the Galapagos Islands, is perfectly adapted to life in the sea. It feeds on algae and has special glands in its nose to excrete excess salt.

Marine iguana

Alligator snapping turtle

Alligator snapping turtles hunt on the bottoms of rivers and lakes. Their dark shells blend in perfectly with the muddy bottoms and weed. When fishing, they open their mouths and wait, attracting prey by means of a worm-like lure near their tongues. Fish swim right into their mouths.

Reptile records

The Asian saltwater crocodile is the largest reptile in the world. Males grow to almost 5 metres long and weigh over 450 kilograms. Tortoises live longer than other reptiles. Many species live to over 100. One of the oldest tortoises recorded died at 152 years of age.

HUNTING TECHNIQUES

Snakes, crocodiles and lizards, and even slow-moving tortoises, are all skillful hunters. Their mouths, jaws, teeth and tongues are specially adapted for hunting.

The **Nile crocodile** is a fearsome predator. It lies in wait under river banks and attacks unsuspecting animals when they come to drink. It drags them into the water and eats them.

Nile crocodile attacking a wildebeest

Snakes' jaws are highly mobile and can open very wide. The **egg-eating snake**, for example, can swallow eggs several times larger than its own head, and the python can gulp down a whole gazelle.

Chameleons have two special adaptations for hunting. Their large eyes function independently, thus increasing their field of vision and the accuracy with which they strike.

15

They also have long elastic tongues, which they flick at insects and spiders. Their tongues have sticky mucus on the end so that when they hit a victim it can't escape.

Common chameleon

SNAKES

Only one-third of all snakes are venomous. The venom, produced by glands in the head, passes into the front fangs from where it is injected into the prey. Pythons, boas and anacondas are not venomous. They suffocate prey by wrapping their bodies around them.

The poisonous **African spitting cobra** can strike at a distance. It can squirt its deadly venom from up to 3 metres away.

African spitting cobra

The **coral snake** has a lethal venom. It can kill a human being. The coral snake's bright colouring serves as a warning to predators, reminding them how dangerous it is.

Coral snake

Anaconda suffocating an alligator

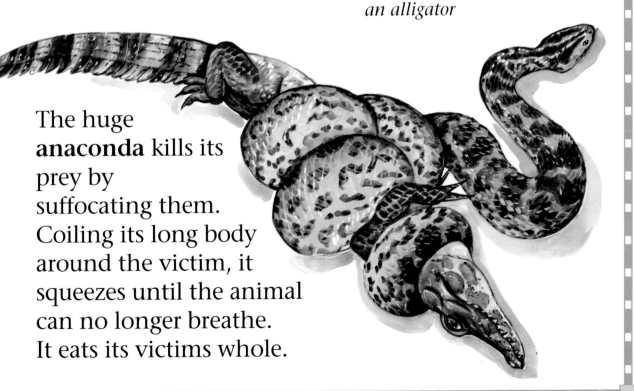

The huge **anaconda** kills its prey by suffocating them. Coiling its long body around the victim, it squeezes until the animal can no longer breathe. It eats its victims whole.

REPRODUCTION

Almost all reptiles lay eggs from which their young hatch. Only a few species give birth to live young. Reptiles, including most aquatic species, nearly always lay their eggs or give birth on land.

Turtle eggs and hatchlings

Redbelly snakes

North American **redbelly snakes** grow inside their mother's body and are born live. They are about 10 centimetres long when they are born.

Many **sea turtles** lay their eggs in nests they dig in the sand. The hatchlings emerge from the sand and run towards the sea. Many are eaten by birds.

Nests and eggs

Reptile eggs have a soft leathery shells. The shell is porous so that the babies inside can breathe. The number of eggs laid varies from one to two hundred, depending on the species. Reptiles usually lay their eggs in nests prepared by the female or hide them under vegetation.

TRANSFORMATIONS

While young reptiles usually increase in size as they grow up, their physical appearance doesn't change. Hatchlings look just as they will as adults, only smaller. Snakes, crocodiles and lizards renew their scaley skins from time to time.

Snakes shed their skins regularly. The old one gradually loosens and they crawl out of it. A fresh, bright skin is already prepared underneath. This is called moulting.

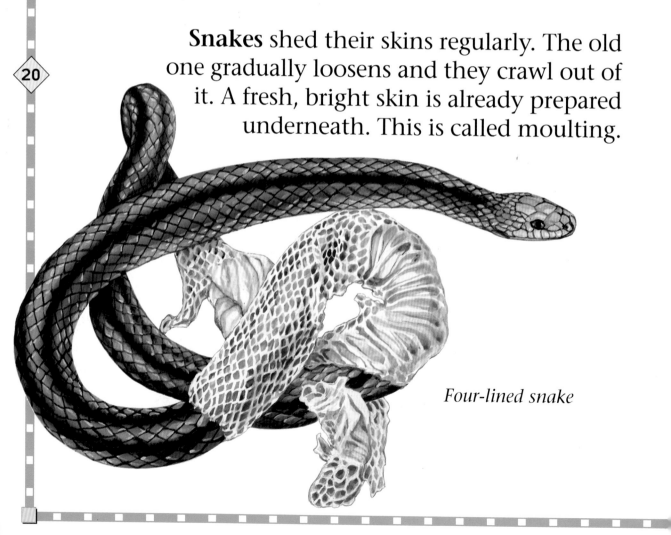

Four-lined snake

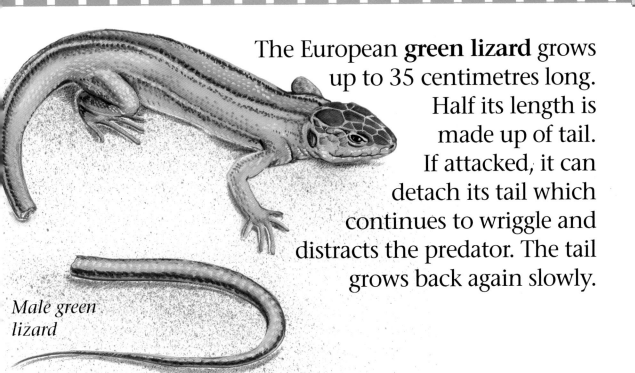

The European **green lizard** grows up to 35 centimetres long. Half its length is made up of tail. If attacked, it can detach its tail which continues to wriggle and distracts the predator. The tail grows back again slowly.

Male green lizard

Turtle hatchlings, like the one shown here riding on its mother's back, look just as they will when they are fully grown. Their shells provide protection from the moment they hatch. The shells get tougher as they grow.

European pond turtles

BLENDING IN

Many reptiles' skins and shells have colours and patterns that blend in so well with their surroundings that they are almost invisible. This helps the animals to hide from predators and to hunt without being seen by their prey.

The **chameleon** can change colour so that it blends into any habitat. To make it even harder to see, it can also take on the shape of a leaf.

Common chameleon

Many tree **snakes** lie in wait for unsuspecting prey, their bodies coiled around the branches. Often they are almost invisible against the foliage. The yellow oil palm snake is very hard to see against the fruit of the oil palm.

Yellow oil palm snake

TYPES OF REPTILES

Scientists divide reptiles into five groups: crocodilians, turtles and tortoises, snakes, lizards, and tuatara. The last group is the smallest. It contains just one species: the tuatara. Lizards constitute the largest group. There are about 3,000 different species.

American banded gecko

The **tuatara** is a living fossil. It descends from a group of reptiles that lived on Earth 135 million years ago. Today it is found only on islands near New Zealand.

Tuatara

Geckos are small lizards.
Active mainly at night, they feed on insects, birds and small mammals. The male gecko makes noises that sound like its name by clicking its tongue against the roof of its mouth. The gecko is the only lizard that can vocalize.

Geckos' feet

Almost all geckos can run up and down steep or vertical surfaces and even zip across ceilings upside-down. They have tiny ridges on the soles of their feet which help them grip onto the tiniest irregularities in the surface, no matter how steep.

REPTILES AND DINOSAURS

The first reptiles appeared on Earth over 280 million years ago. Several million years later, a group of reptiles called dinosaurs came to dominate life on Earth. Dinosaurs became extinct about 65 million years ago.

Komodo dragon

The **Komodo dragon** is the largest living lizard. It can grow up to 3 metres in length. It is an active hunter and will attack and kill prey as large as pigs and deer. It has also been known to kill humans.

Basilisks are a type of lizard. Over short distances they can run in an upright position on their back legs. They can also scoot across the surface of the water.

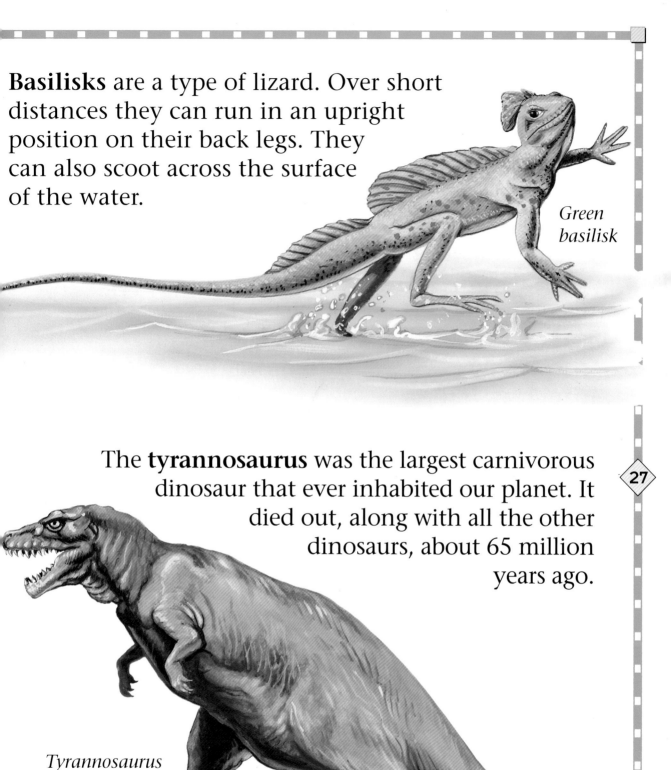

Green basilisk

The **tyrannosaurus** was the largest carnivorous dinosaur that ever inhabited our planet. It died out, along with all the other dinosaurs, about 65 million years ago.

Tyrannosaurus

INDEX